Let's launch into this book . . .

First Published 2025 by Jenny Dyer
For further information
contact through facebook page

Walking with Wildlife

or website

www.walkingwithwildlife.com.au

Text: © Jennifer Dyer 2025
Photography: © Jennifer Dyer 2024-25

All rights reserved. No part of this publication may be reproduced, stored in a retrieval system, or transmitted in any form or by any means electronic or mechanical, or by photocopying or otherwise without prior written permission of the author or copyright holder.

Soft Cover ISBN 978-1-7640280-3-5
Hard Cover ISBN 978-1-7640280-4-2

Cover and Artwork: Jenny Dyer

Walking with Wildlife™

BOOK 8 - SNACK TIME

Written by Jenny Dyer
Photography and Design by Jenny Dyer

I was just getting ready for my early morning walk when I heard the unmistakable racket of a juvenile channel-billed cuckoo outside. I raced to get my camera and followed the noise to obtain a photo.

The last thing I expected was this crow to land on the branch beside it and start feeding the foster fledgling.

I had no time to do anything but snap. No time to zoom out to frame the bird better.

The channel-billed cuckoos lay their eggs in another bird's nest (in this case the crow's nest) and expect them to keep the eggs warm until they hatch. The crows here then raised the three massive channel-billed cuckoo babies. An awesome effort!

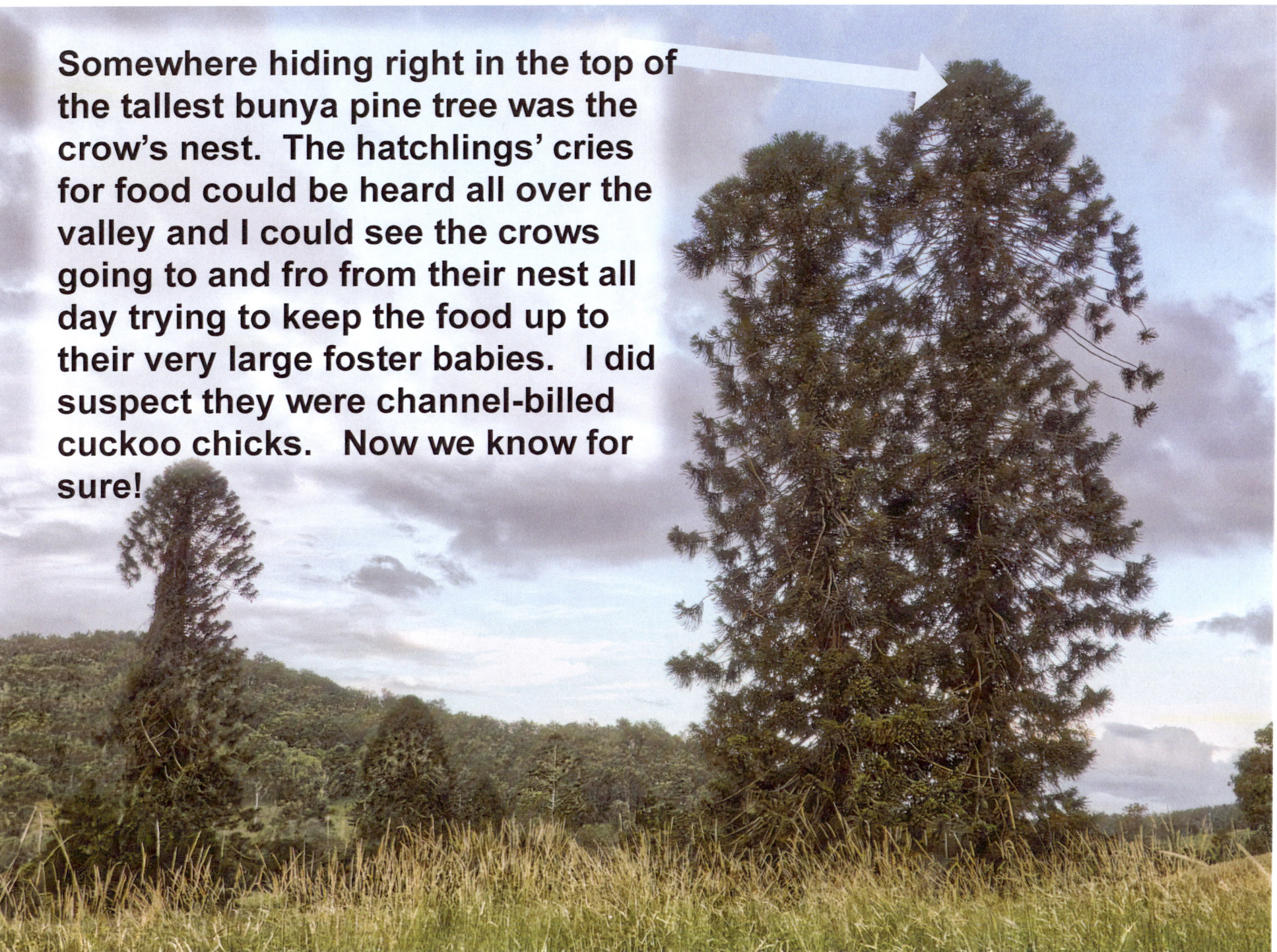

Somewhere hiding right in the top of the tallest bunya pine tree was the crow's nest. The hatchlings' cries for food could be heard all over the valley and I could see the crows going to and fro from their nest all day trying to keep the food up to their very large foster babies. I did suspect they were channel-billed cuckoo chicks. Now we know for sure!

When the channel-billed cuckoo fledglings left the nest, they were hanging around with the crows making loud noises all over our little valley, as they were still expecting to be fed. I caught this photo in a bunya tree. Those trees are so spiky. You have to be very careful walking under them as they drop those sharp leaves everywhere.

We've been out and about watching these birds for ages. My two grandchildren and I lined up this photo of the channel-billed cuckoo who was eating berries from a cedar tree. These berries are poisonous or toxic for humans but birds can eat them. The birds also love figs and insects. We have so much fun bird-watching together!

I had to zoom in a long way to capture this photo. I reckon these birds were surveying the landscape for places to lay their eggs. They are very good detectives to be able to find an established nest to lay their eggs in, as well as obtaining good foster parents for their young.

That was the last morning I had a chance to photograph the channel-billed cuckoos before they migrated north to Indonesian or Papua New Guinea for winter. What a relief for the crows! They must have been exhausted keeping food up to the three large foster babies. I wonder if the cuckoos will do the same thing next year.

Crows enjoy a meal of cane toad. They turn them upside down and eat their bellies out avoiding the skin where the poison is.

The cane toad is an imported pest that was supposed to eat the grey cane beetle which was affecting the sugar cane fields. They were ineffective at controlling the beetle but then quickly spread over Australia. They have poisonous skin and can actually squirt white poison out of these glands at the side of their necks when threatened.

The cane toads were in plague proportions and poisoned a lot of wildlife until birds learnt how to eat them without dying.

Wow! A goanna just raced across the track in front of me and climbed a tree!

Just look at that swagger on the goanna as he heads for safety in the treetop and as soon as he climbed up, the birds started squawking, announcing his presence to all the other birds.

That hitch-hiker on his head is living dangerously, or is he?

If you hear a lot of noise like birds squawking loudly, it usually means there's a predator like a goanna or raptor around. Goannas (or lace monitors) love eggs and hatchlings.

The brown falcon has been hanging around the water hole in the gully. I saw him up in the tree scanning his surroundings. He flew down quickly but to my surprise this time when he flew back up, HE had a surprise.

He was carrying a red-belly black snake he caught. (Also see book cover). How cool is that!

The raptors love to eat small animals and birds, insects and reptiles. They are carnivores, meaning they are meat eaters. Can you find any other carnivores in this book?

Talk about a noisy morning! I could hear the sulphur-crested cockatoos very clearly. They are the loudest bird in the world. I could see them in the bunya trees, which are a great source of food for them when the nuts are in season. How they land on those spiky trees, I don't know!

In comes the second one for a graceful landing. Then they settle into eating bunya nuts.

The cockatoo is holding a nut in one foot and breaking it with his strong beak. When ripe, you can hear the large pods come crashing to the ground. Each pod is about 40 cm long and contains about 100 nuts. The heavy pods have been know to kill cows standing under the trees.

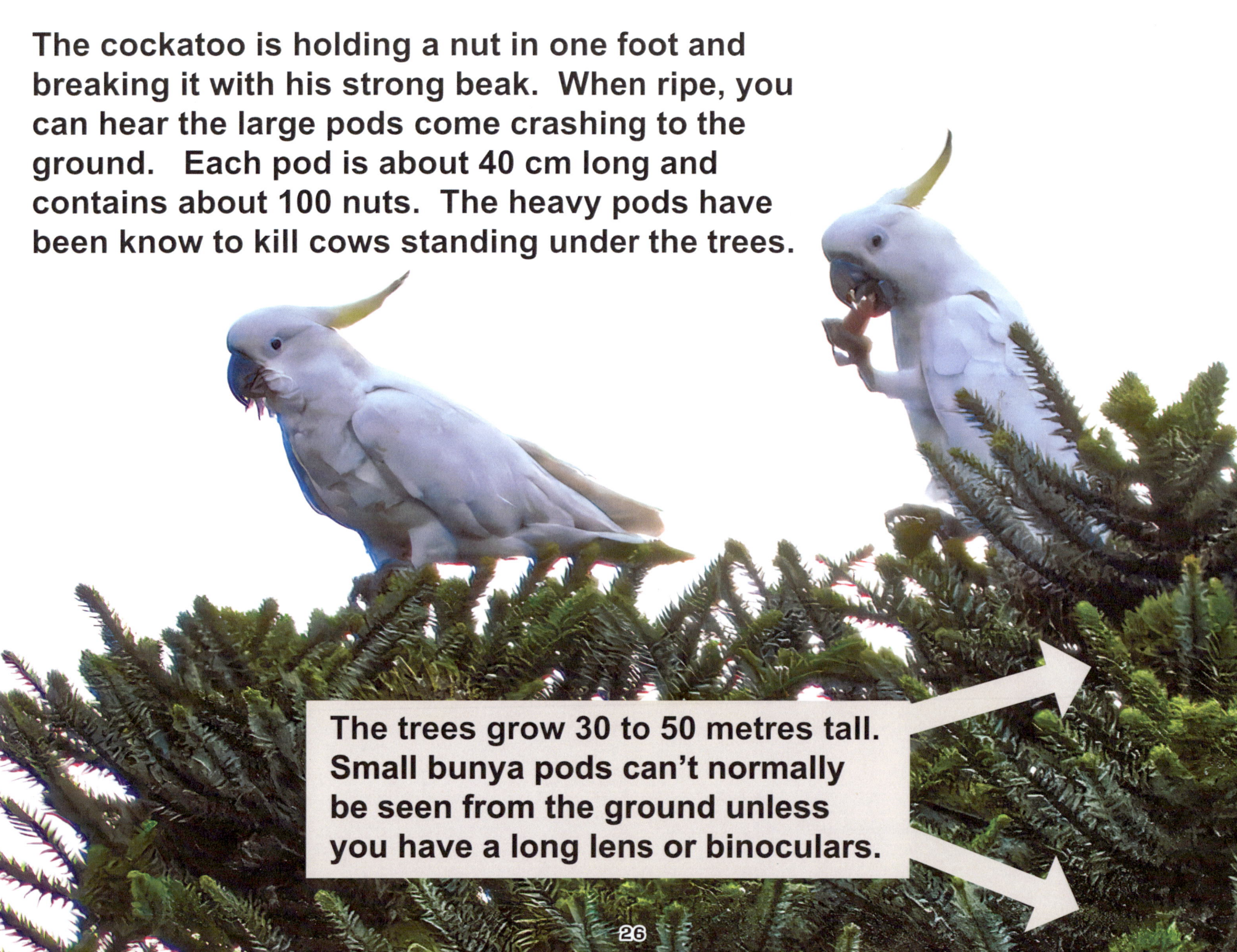

The trees grow 30 to 50 metres tall. Small bunya pods can't normally be seen from the ground unless you have a long lens or binoculars.

This is the big tree they were sitting in.

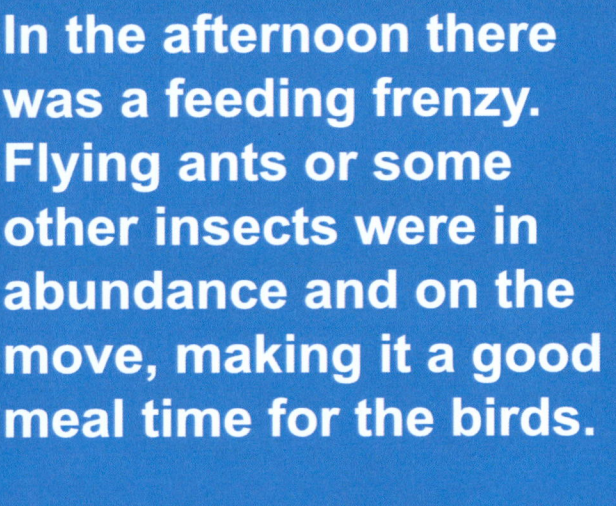

In the afternoon there was a feeding frenzy. Flying ants or some other insects were in abundance and on the move, making it a good meal time for the birds.

The blue-faced honeyeaters were certainly very busy chasing them. They must have very good eyesight because I couldn't see the insects. The birds were going this way then that. Too quick for me.

Look at him concentrating on his next meal.

Why do you think his tongue is hanging out? Did you know they have very sticky tongues which can be used for gathering nectar or insects?

The grey butcherbird was also in on the act. There were birds everywhere!

I didn't know which way to point my camera!

This noisy friarbird was also watching closely.

Later, I captured a pied butcherbird throwing an insect in the air and down it goes in less that half a second. I know because my camera takes seven photos a second and the insect was gone in two photos.

The grey butcherbird on the opposite page is enjoying a grub in the undercover.

I love the chatter of the pale-headed rosellas. I could hear them coming in near our place in the late afternoon. These little birds were enjoying a snack on our overgrown lawn.

They also eat berries. They are herbivores which means they feed mainly on plant life.

Grass seed is a favourite. You'll sometimes see them on fences but more often they take off very quickly and will be gone before you can photograph them.

Even though they have bright colours they are well camouflaged.

This forest kingfisher sat up on the electrical wire waiting to spot a meal.

Yes! He caught a grasshopper. He gave it a beating on the wire.

He then threw it into the air and down the hatch it goes, just like that.

This kookaburra (another member of the kingfisher family) is enjoying a meal of praying mantis in much the same way.

What! A very small praying mantis enjoying an even smaller meal of some insect.

He'd better hide from the kingfishers and kookaburras or he'll be breakfast for them!

Here is a much larger praying mantis ready to make a rapid strike with his front legs.

Another feeding frenzy - this time near the gully, and the red-backed fairy wrens weren't noticing me. There was too much food around for them.

This male red-backed fairy wren gulped the whole praying mantis down in less than half a second.

Meanwhile. the peaceful doves pick up tiny seeds from the ground. Too small to see with your eyes.

www.ingramcontent.com/pod-product-compliance
Lightning Source LLC
Chambersburg PA
CBRC101356070526
44583CB00010B/197